FILMS AND SPECIAL EFFECTS

Susan Meredith and Phil Mottram

Contents

Designed by Roger Priddy

Illustrated by

Kuo Kang Chen, Jeremy Banks, Graham Round,
Jeremy Gower, Oliver Frey, Diana Stevens,
Rob McCaig and Sue Stitt

Film tricks

The films you see in the cinema usually tell a story and are often called feature films. There are many other types of film, including factual or "documentary" films, films made specially for television and home movies. What all the types have in common is that the pictures are recorded and stored on film. The pictures of "videos" and most television programmes are stored on tape. In this book you will find out mainly how films for the cinema are made. These are the type which have the most special effects.

Special effects are techniques used to trick the audience into believing they are seeing something which they really are not. They are used when the pictures the film-makers want cannot be created in the normal way because it is either impossible, or too expensive or dangerous. Science fiction and disaster films, in particular, have lots of special effects. Later in the book you can find out how many of the spectacular large-scale effects are produced. On these pages are some examples of other, less complicated tricks which are used all the time to help convince you that what you are seeing is really happening.

How films work

Films are known as "movies" because the pictures you see on the screen appear to move. In reality though they do not move at all. What you are really seeing is a series of still photographs projected on to the screen in rapid succession so that they look as though they are moving.

You do not notice the change-over from one picture to the next because of the way your eyes work. Whenever you stop looking at one thing and look at another, your eyes do not react immediately but, for a fraction of a second, continue to see the original scene. This phenomenon is called "persistence of vision". Without it the photographs on the cinema screen would not blend smoothly into one another to make one continuous picture. In the clip of film on the left, you can see that the car is in a slightly different position in each photograph. When these are projected in rapid succession, the car appears to go into the tunnel.

Each individual photograph is called a "frame" of film. Usually 24 frames are projected every second. To make the action appear at natural speed, the camera has to take the same number of frames per second during filming.

The first films

1 Many special effects are made possible because of the way a film consists of individual photographs. Effects were used even in the earliest films, made in the 1890s.* One of the first film-makers was a French magician called Georges Méliès. In his film *Cinderella*, made in 1899, he transformed a pumpkin into Cinderella's coach simply by stopping the camera during filming and substituting the coach for the pumpkin between frames. This is known as a jump cut and is still used today to make things vanish into thin air or appear from nowhere.

2 In real life certain actions take place too fast for the human eye to register all the details. If a film of a rapid action is projected at a slower speed than it was photographed, the action appears in slow motion and it is then possible to see the details. Early films settled long-standing disagreements about movement, for example whether a trotting horse lifts all four feet off the ground at once.

Sets

The scenery, or "sets", for a film can be built to look very realistic by skilled craftspeople. They are not always as elaborate as they look though. Nor are they necessarily even the same way up as they appear on the screen. For example, the simplest way to produce a joke scene of someone dancing on a ceiling is to build the set upside down and turn the camera upside down during filming.

Lenses

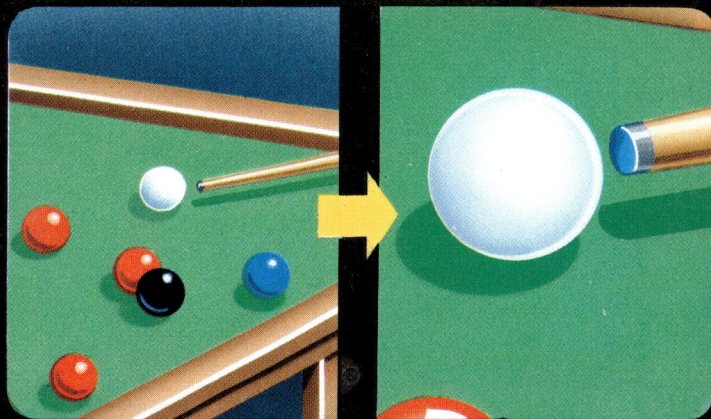

Different types of lens are used on the camera to produce different types of picture. One of the most important is the zoom lens. With a zoom, the camera operator can enlarge or reduce whatever is in the picture, such as this snooker table, without stopping the camera between frames and without moving it. This makes the audience feel as though they are zooming in towards the table or zooming out away from it.

Lights

To create the precise effect the film-makers want, artificial lights are used not only to illuminate the sets indoors but almost always outdoors as well, even on sunny days. This means that the weather you see on the screen is rarely completely true-to-life. The canopy shown in the picture above is to cut out glare from the sun.

Sometimes lighting and other devices are used to make it look as though it is a different time of day. Some night scenes, for example, are filmed in daylight, using a partly grey glass filter on the camera. The grey part of the filter is positioned over the camera's view of the sky to make it look darker. This is called day-for-night filming.

Make-up

Older

Younger

Make-up is used all the time in films to alter people's appearance. To age someone, shadows and wrinkles are painted on, grey powder is put in the hair and bald patches can be created using a thin rubber wig called a skin. Caps can be made for the teeth to make them look rotten and pads of cotton wool put in the mouth to make the face fatter.

To make someone look younger, a facelift is sometimes necessary. Patches of muslin with threads attached are stuck on the cheeks. The threads are then tied on top of the head to pull the skin tight under the chin. The threads are hidden by the hairstyle or a wig and the muslin patches are covered with make-up.

How films are made

There are many different processes involved in making a film. Some of them take place simultaneously, so good organization and co-ordination between the different people involved are essential. You can see how many people work on a film just by looking at the long list of credits at the end. Some full-length feature films take several years to make and cost millions of pounds.

You can find out more about the different processes described here later in the book.

1 Production

The entire production of the film is supervised by a producer. The producer raises the money needed, commissions a script, hires the director, actors and technicians, and sells the finished film. The initial idea for the film may come from the producer, director or script-writer.

2 Script

A script-writer produces a script, or "screenplay", for the film. This describes the action and the settings, and gives the actors' dialogue. The screenplay is later broken down into a more detailed "shooting script" to be followed during filming.

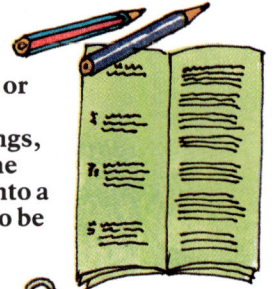

6 Shooting

The scenes are filmed, or "shot", under the supervision of the director. They are usually shot out of sequence and often need several "takes" to get them right. On average only about ten per cent of the film shot is used in the finished film. A whole day's shooting sometimes produces only about three minutes of screen time.

Microphone

Camera

8 Processing

Developing machinery

The film is processed in special laboratories. The pictures taken during shooting are developed to produce "negatives" and then printed on to another piece of film to produce "positives". These first positive prints are used for editing the film while the negatives are kept safe. The prints are called "rushes" because they are rushed to the director and editor for checking every day during shooting.

9 Editing

Editing machine

An editor chooses the best takes of the different scenes and puts the film together in the right order. The different sound recordings are also edited before being mixed together into one master soundtrack. The director is almost always involved in the editing.

3 Art department

The sets, costumes and properties ("props") needed for the film are made in the art department under the supervision of the art director.

4 Special effects

Some effects, such as fires or car crashes, are created during filming, often using skilled stunt artists. Some are prepared separately, in model-making "shops" like the one above, for example. Others are created after filming, while the film is being processed at the laboratories.

5 Animation

For animated (cartoon) films or sequences, a whole series of pictures is individually drawn and then photographed. Computers are sometimes used to do the drawings.

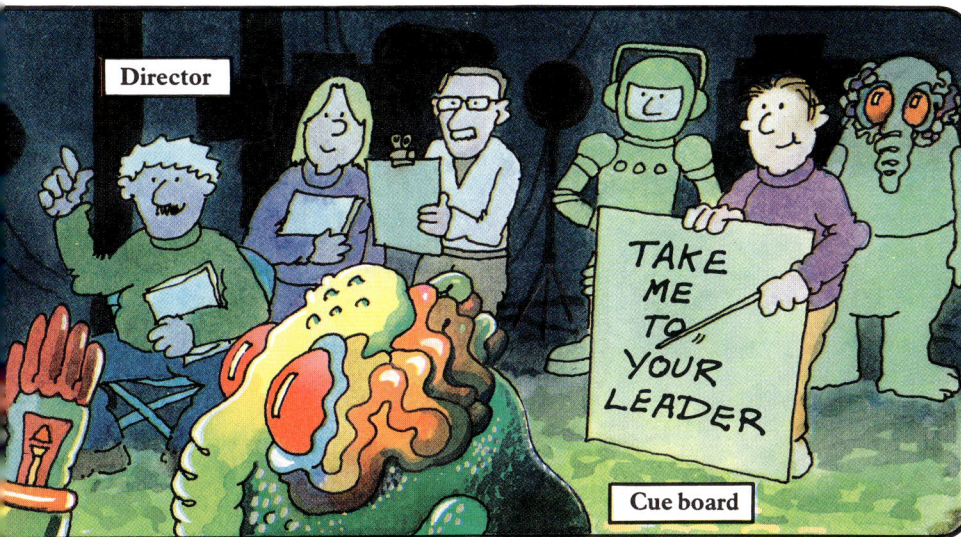

Director

TAKE ME TO YOUR LEADER

Cue board

7 Sound

The sound is first recorded on tape and then transferred to film. Usually only the dialogue is recorded while the pictures are being shot. All the other sounds are recorded separately. Later, all the soundtracks are mixed into one and put on to the same film as the pictures.

10 Printing

Printing machine

The edited film goes back to the laboratories and the negatives are cut to match it. The master soundtrack is converted into an "optical sound negative". This means that the sound is stored as a photographic pattern on film. (Optical means "to do with sight".) The picture negatives and the sound negative are then printed together on to one piece of film to produce a positive, "married" print.

11 Distribution

SPACE LOVE

The producer has made contracts with film distributors. They book the film into cinemas and organize the publicity for it.

12 In the cinema

Identical copies of the married print are shown in cinemas, using projectors. The prints can also be transferred to video tape or cassette for broadcasting on TV or showing on home video equipment.

In a film studio

Some of the shooting for most films takes place in a studio. The most important part of a studio complex is the "sound stage" (shown here). This is where the pictures are shot and the dialogue is recorded. Major studios have several different departments, including carpentry and plaster shops where the sets are built, a properties department where furniture and other objects needed for the sets are assembled, a wardrobe department where the costumes are made, and a make-up department. A production manager makes sure that everything needed for a shooting session is in the right place at the right time.

The lamps usually hang from rails over the set. They can be raised, lowered or moved along the rails automatically. Their angle can be adjusted either by hand from a catwalk above the set or with poles from the ground.

Thick, solid walls help to make the studio sound-proof. The walls of the sound stage are lined with sound-absorbing material to prevent echo. If the set is meant to be a small room, sound-absorbent screens may be used around the floor and sound-absorbent panels over the top.

The camera is often mounted on a wheeled platform called a dolly. The camera can be raised or lowered. This is known as craning. It can also be tilted, and turned to left or right. The sideways movement is called panning. The dolly can be moved during shots. This is known as tracking because it is sometimes done on special tracks like miniature railway lines.

A "clapperboard" is used to number the different shots so they can easily be identified during editing. At the start of each shot, one of the camera crew, called the "clapper", holds the board up in front of the camera with the numbers of the shot and the take chalked on it. The clapper shouts out the numbers and claps the stick against the top of the board so the sound it makes is recorded on the dialogue track. During editing, the shots and takes can be identified just by looking at the film. The sound can be matched up with the pictures by matching the spot on the sound film where the clapstick is heard with the frame of picture film where the stick is seen hitting the board.

The camera has a team or "crew" of several people to work it. The one in charge is called the lighting camera person or director of photography and works closely with the director. The person who looks through the viewfinder and pans and tilts the camera is called the operator. The people who push the dolly around and control craning are known as "grips".

If a scene is meant to be outdoors, a large piece of canvas is often used as a backdrop to the set. This is painted a plain colour to look like the sky and is called a skycloth or cyclorama. Sometimes a giant photograph or painting of buildings or scenery is used as the backdrop.

The audience must not be able to tell that the scenes have been filmed bit by bit and out of order. A "continuity person" makes detailed notes and takes photographs during the shooting sessions to make sure that no mistakes of continuity creep in. An example would be a clock showing an earlier time at the end of a scene than at the beginning.

Some weather effects are created in the studio. For example, overhead spray pipes can be used for rain.

Large electric fans are used for making wind and granules of foam polystyrene can be dropped for snow.

A machine which makes smoke or steam is used to give the effect of mist or fog.

The microphone is often attached to a long rod called a boom. A "boom swinger" adjusts the length of the rod and positions the microphone close to whichever actor is speaking, taking care to keep it just out of the picture.

Filming is supervised by the director, who gives instructions to the actors and camera crew. The director works from the shooting script, which gives details of how each shot should be filmed and sometimes includes even the camera movements. A shot is any part of a scene that can be filmed without stopping the camera. It is the director who decides how many takes each shot needs before it is right.

Part of the floor can be lifted up to make a pit for the camera if a shot needs to be filmed from a low angle. Pits can also be filled with water for shots of, for example, someone falling in a river. For underwater shots, a special tank is built and the camera films through windows in the side.

How the camera works

There are four main types of film camera. The one shown here is the type used for making most feature films. It is called a 35mm camera because it takes film which is 35mm wide. Spectacular feature films are sometimes made using a 65mm camera, which takes film 65mm wide. 16mm cameras are used for filming documentaries and many TV programmes and 8mm cameras are used for making home movies.

All film cameras work in a similar way and on the same basic principle as an ordinary, still camera. Light from a scene goes through the lens or "eye" of the camera and causes an invisible chemical change in the film which is behind the lens. When the film is developed, an image of the scene becomes visible. After being printed, this picture can be projected on to a screen.

Lens

Focus set by turning this ring.

Zoom control

Exposure set by turning this ring.

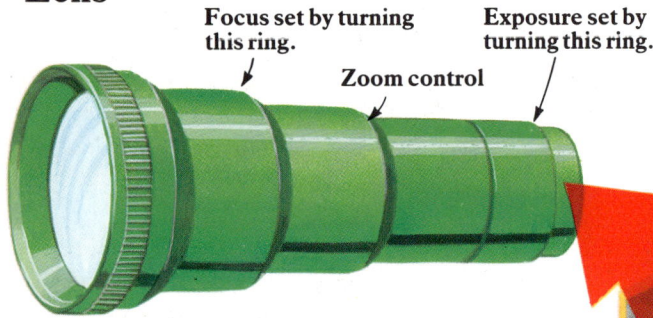

The camera lens is a specially designed piece of glass inside this case or "barrel". The size of the lens opening or "aperture" can be altered to let in the right amount of light for the conditions and the type of film being used. This is called setting the exposure.

The lens can be moved closer to or further from the film, depending on the distance of the camera from the objects being photographed. This is called focusing and is necessary to get the picture clear and sharp.

Matte box

This shades the lens to stop too much light going into the camera and is used in creating certain special effects. You can find out more about these on pages 14-15.

Focus control

This control turns the focus ring on the lens. It is operated by a member of the crew called the focus puller. On some cameras the focus puller operates the knob by remote control.

Shutter

Lens

Shutter

Film

Register pins

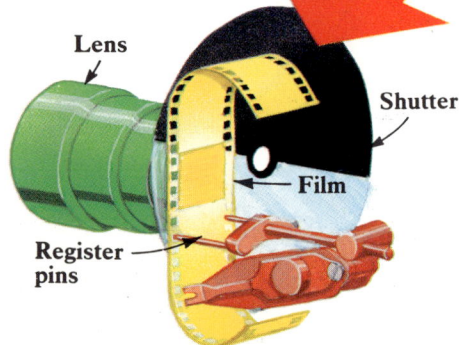

This is a semicircular metal disc which rotates between the lens and the film. The shutter covers the film while it is moving through the camera and exposes it when it is stationary behind the lens. The exposure time is usually 1/50th of a second.

Inside the camera

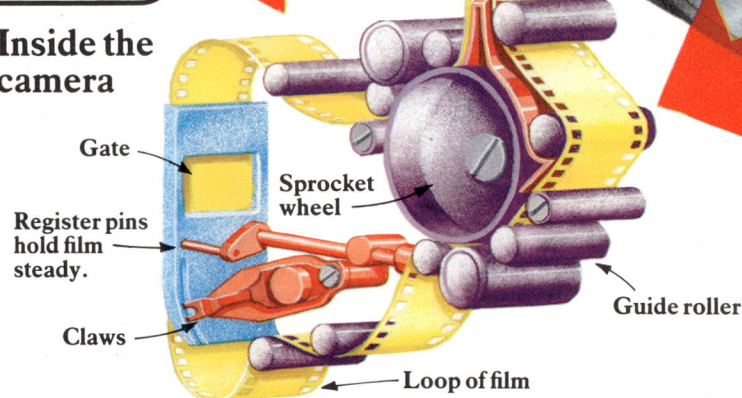

Gate

Register pins hold film steady.

Sprocket wheel

Claws

Guide roller

Loop of film

The film is drawn through the camera by a revolving sprocket wheel. It is pulled down behind the lens in a series of jerks by steel "claws". These fit into the perforations (tiny holes) at the sides of the film. When a piece of film is framed in the "gate" behind the lens, the claws retract. Register pins are then inserted to hold the film steady while the picture is taken. Usually 24 frames are taken every second. So that the film does not get pulled taut and break, two slack loops are left above and below the gate.

Magazine

The film is stored on reels, or spools, in a light-proof "magazine". It is drawn through the camera from the feed spool to the take-up spool. The film has to be loaded into the magazine in a darkroom or special "changing bag" so that no light falls on it. A member of the crew called the loader has special responsibility for this.

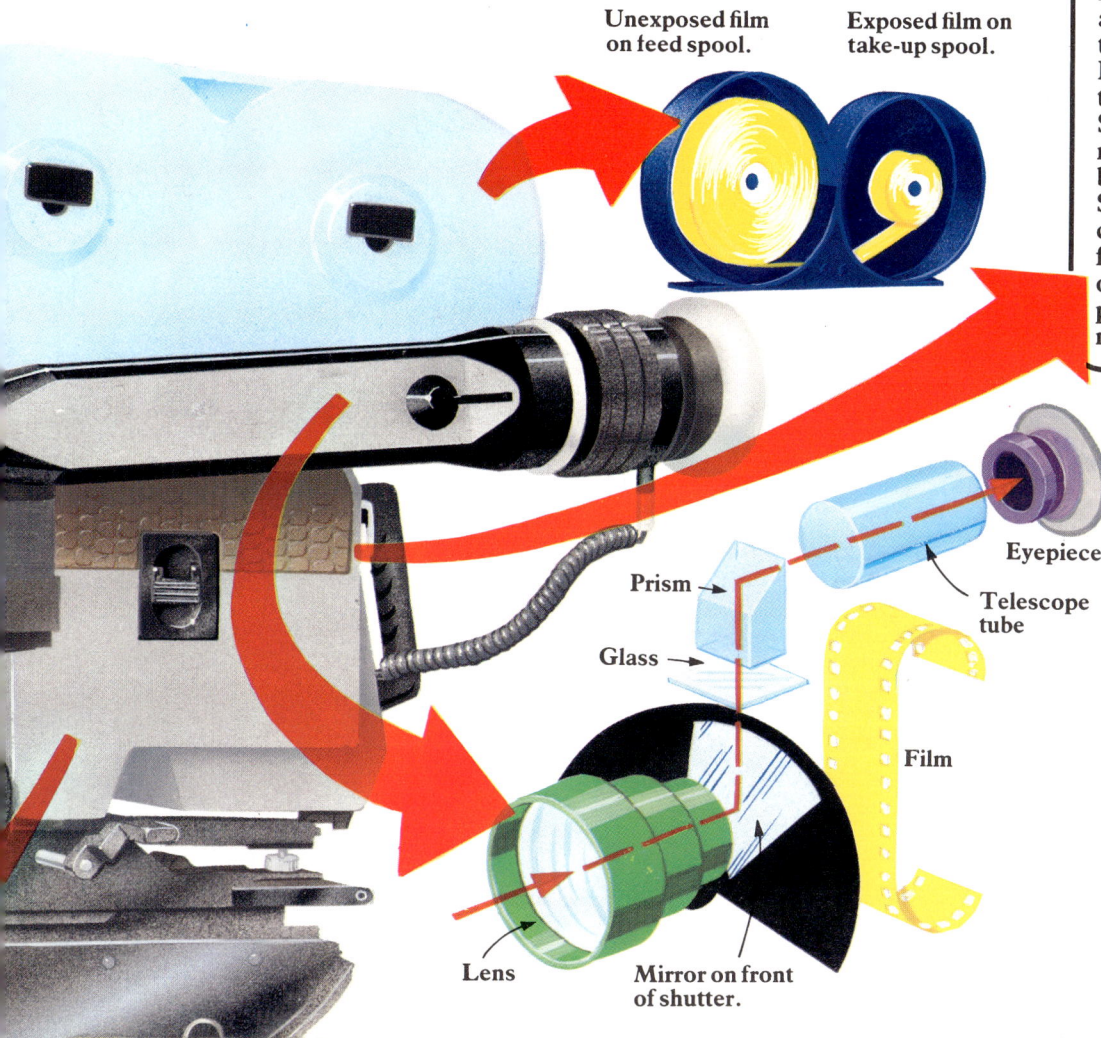

Unexposed film on feed spool.

Exposed film on take-up spool.

Motor

The camera is driven by an electric motor. The speed of the motor is usually the same as the speed of the motor which will project the finished film. If a film is projected at a slower speed than it was shot, the action appears in slow motion. If it is projected at a faster speed, the action appears speeded up. Slow motion is sometimes used to make violent scenes look more bloodthirsty and long-drawn-out. Speeding up is usually used for comic effect or to add excitement, for example to a car chase. Some old films look speeded up because projectors run at faster speeds nowadays than they used to.

Viewfinder

This allows the camera operator to see what is being shot. A mirror on the front of the rotating shutter reflects the scene on to a piece of glass when the shutter is closed. A prism and a magnifying telescope tube allow the operator to see the scene on the glass. When the shutter is open, all the light goes on to the film for the picture to be taken.

Some large cameras have a miniature TV camera attached to the viewfinder. This scans the picture reflected on to the glass and relays it to a screen and video recorder for the director to view and re-play.

Prism

Glass

Eyepiece

Telescope tube

Film

Lens

Mirror on front of shutter.

What is film?

Unexposed film, known as "raw stock".

Perforation

Silver halide crystals (magnified).

Cinema film is made of a thin plastic called cellulose acetate. On one side it has a coating of gelatin containing tiny crystals of silver halide. These crystals change when they are exposed to light. The most common widths of film are 35mm, 65mm, 16mm and 8mm. 65mm film is enlarged to 70mm during printing.

How a lens works

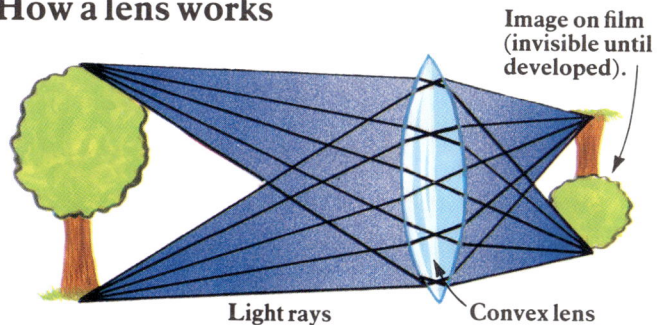

Image on film (invisible until developed).

Light rays

Convex lens

Light is constantly being reflected by objects in all directions. When rays of light go into a camera lens, the convex (outward-curving) surfaces of the lens bend the rays inwards. The rays cross each other behind the lens. This produces a small photographic image upside down on the light-sensitive film.

Outside the studio

There are various reasons for filming outside a studio. One is that it is difficult to get a realistic outdoor effect when filming indoors. Some film-makers prefer to go to real places even for indoor scenes.

Filming away from the studio, whether outdoors or in, is called filming on location. Another alternative, for outdoor scenes, is to film on the "lot". This is a huge uncovered area within the studio complex.

Hose

On the lot

One advantage of filming on the lot is that all the usual studio facilities are on hand. If the weather makes shooting outdoors impossible, any studio scenes can be filmed instead.

An important feature of many lots is the enormous water tank. The edges of the tank can be covered with mud and plants to look like a river bank or with tons of sand to look like the sea-shore. The tank is useful when violent weather effects are needed. High winds can be created using powerful aeroplane propellers and torrents of rain are produced by aiming hoses into the air. Waves are made by wave-making machinery of the type used in swimming pools. The tank is also used for filming models of ships.

A huge painted wall behind the water tank is used as a skycloth.

Scaffolding

Wave machine

For some scenes only a fairly simple set, like this cliff, is needed but the lot is large enough for entire streets to be built on it. Sometimes exact copies of real streets are made in wood and plaster.

Dump tank

On location

A great deal of filming is done on location because of the ready-made realistic settings this provides. There are certain disadvantages though. First, a lot of organization and expense is involved in transporting all the people and equipment to the location. Almost all the studio facilities are needed, including the camera, lighting and sound equipment, props, costumes and make-up. Once at the location, certain alterations usually have to be made to make the place exactly right for the film. For a historical film, for instance, these include taking down the TV aerials and covering traffic signs and parking meters. During shooting, streets may have to be closed to traffic and members of the public. Background noise, of birds, aircraft or the wind, for example, almost always means that the sound has to be re-recorded later in a studio. Also, a lot of time can be spent waiting for the right sort of weather.

Propeller

Parking meter disguised as water pump.

When a flood or tidal wave is needed, the "dump" tank is used. This is above the main water tank and holds hundreds of gallons of water. When the tank is tipped, a deluge of water pours down into the main tank.

Lighting and make-up

The type of lighting used in a film affects its whole look and atmosphere. In a comedy or musical, for example, the sets are usually brightly lit to give a cheerful, sunny atmosphere. This is called high key lighting. For mystery and horror films shadows are created to make the atmosphere tense and creepy. This is called low key lighting. Continuity in lighting is important. All the shots in one sequence, and sometimes throughout the whole film, have to have the same quality of light so that their order can be altered during editing.

Make-up is always planned in conjunction with lighting because lights affect the appearance of make-up. One of the main purposes of film make-up, besides creating character or making someone look glamorous, is to ensure continuity. It covers up any natural variations in the actors' complexions during the time it takes to complete the shooting.

Here is a simple lighting set-up of the type that might be used for an indoor scene on location. The electricians who set up the lights are called "sparks". The chief electrician is often known as the "gaffer".

3 Other lamps light the set around the actors. They are often used to cast interesting shadows on walls.

4 A backlight or "rim" light above and behind the actors helps to make them stand out from the background and highlights their hair.

1 The main light on the actors is called the key light. The position of the shutters, or "barn doors", on the lamp head can be altered to mask off parts of the light. Outdoors the sun often acts as the key light, with lamps used to supplement it.

2 The strong key light often casts hard shadows. A secondary light, called a filler, is used to shine soft light into the shadows and fill them in.

Outdoors, the sun itself can sometimes be used as the filler. It is reflected into the shadows by boards covered with aluminium foil.

5 To make the actors look glamorous, a tiny lamp called a catchlight may be positioned on the camera. This is reflected in their eyes and teeth so they appear to shine.

Masks

Make-up alone is not enough to bring about some dramatic changes that are needed. To turn an actor into a monster, the make-up artist usually has to make a mask.

1 A mould is made of the actor's face by coating it with plaster. When the plaster has set, the mould is taken off and liquid plaster is poured into it. When the liquid plaster has set, the mould is removed and a model of the actor's face is left.

2 The make-up artist constructs the mask on the plaster model. This is usually done by painting liquid latex on to it. The latex dries out as a thin layer of rubber. It can be built up with padding and given a rough surface by incorporating sawdust.

3 The end result is a flexible mask which fits the actor's face perfectly. It can be stuck on with glue and feels hot and uncomfortable. It may include false eyes, lumps and scars. Thick masks sometimes contain strings the actor can pull to produce movements such as frowning or raising the eyebrows. When the mask is in position, make-up is used on top.

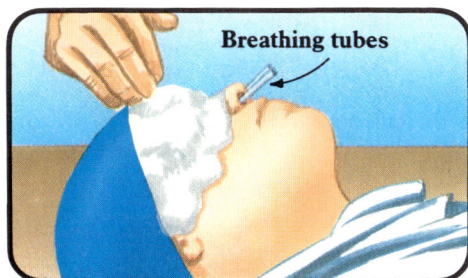

Breathing tubes

Film sound

The sound for a film is first recorded on tape, using a microphone and a high-quality portable recorder. Then it is transferred to film so it can be edited alongside the pictures. Finally, it is put on to the same piece of film as the pictures.

The sound of the actors' dialogue has to match up, or "synchronize", with the lip movements seen on the screen, so this is recorded at the same time as the pictures are shot. Other sounds, such as effects and music, are recorded separately ("wild"), or are obtained from special sound libraries.

The film used for home movies usually has a specially prepared magnetic stripe down one side and the sound is recorded straight on to this, while shooting is taking place. This makes editing the sound more complicated.

Microphones

1 One of the main difficulties in recording sound for films is to avoid picking up unwanted background noise, such as the camera motor or, outside the studio, traffic. For this reason, "directional" or "cardioid" microphones are often used. These pick up sound from the front only, rather than from all around. Attaching the microphone to a boom means it can be positioned very close to the sound while still being kept out of the picture.

Dubbing

1 Dummy door with different latches and locks.

2 Watering can for sound of light shower of rain.

3 Film counter

Playback machine

Recorder

4 Water tank for splashing noises.

5 Sound of fire is made by crinkling cellophane paper near microphone.

6 Slashing a cabbage with a heavy knife can sound like a stabbing.

7 Footsteps are produced by specialized technicians walking on different surfaces.

8 Gunshots, explosions, ray gun sounds are sometimes produced by an electronic effects generator.

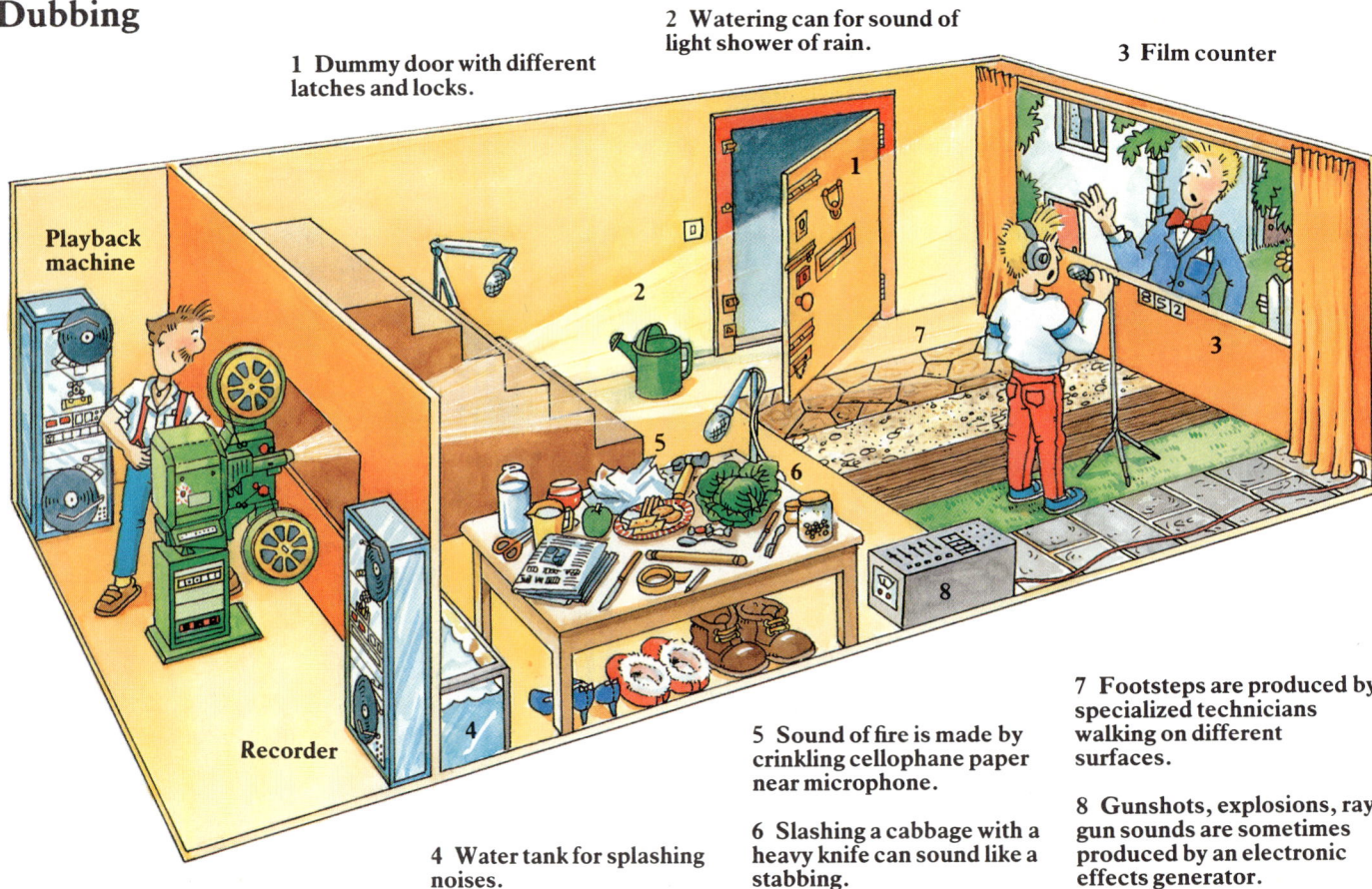

If a recording made while shooting is too poor to use, because of background noise, for example, the sound has to be re-recorded, or "dubbed", in a studio like the one above. Dialogue recorded on location almost always has to be dubbed. As the pictures are projected on to a screen in the studio, the actors speak the words again, "in sync" with the lip movements, and a new recording is made. The original track is played back over the actors' headphones as a guide. Both this and the picture film are cut into short circular loops which can be repeated several times for practice. Sometimes completely different actors are used to do the dubbing.

If sound effects are not already available on tape or record, some, such as those shown above, can be recorded in the dubbing studio in sync with the pictures. Background music too is sometimes recorded in the studio with the musicians playing to the pictures. Films can be converted into foreign languages by dubbing.

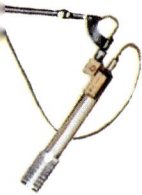

Neck-mike

Cable

1
How the sound is recorded

When someone makes a noise, sound waves are produced in the air. A microphone has a sensitive metal disc called a diaphragm inside it. When sound waves hit the diaphragm, they make it vibrate. A device attached to the diaphragm turns the vibrations into electric signals. The signals vary according to the sounds.

Diaphragm

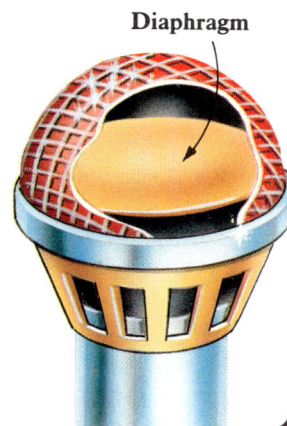

2 Sometimes, if it is inconvenient to use a boom, the actors have a small "neck-mike" concealed in their clothes. If it is not possible to have a cable leading from the actor to the tape recorder, the microphone may be attached to a small radio transmitter which is hidden in the actor's pocket. The sound signals then travel to the recorder through the air on radio waves. A disadvantage of neck-mikes is that rustling sounds are often picked up as the actors move around.

2

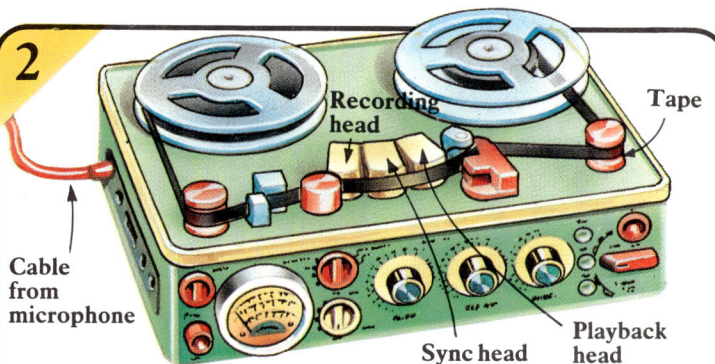

Recording head

Tape

Cable from microphone

Sync head

Playback head

The sound signals go down a cable to the recording head of a tape recorder. Tape, which is coated with millions of tiny particles of iron oxide, passes across the head. The sound signals magnetize the particles of iron oxide. The sound is now stored on tape as a magnetic pattern and can be played back over loudspeakers or fed to another machine for re-recording.

The recorders used for film sound have an extra head, called a "sync" head. Electric pulses are fed from the camera motor to the sync head and are recorded on the tape. These pulses register the frames of film as they pass through the camera so the sound and pictures can be synchronized.

3 If there is a great deal of background noise, or it is impossible to get very close to the sound, on location for example, a gun microphone can be used. These are super-cardioid, which means they can pick up sound from quite a distance away provided the microphone is pointed in exactly the right direction.

3

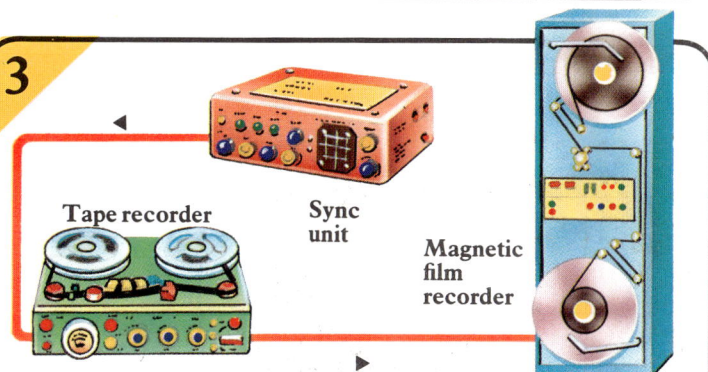

Tape recorder

Sync unit

Magnetic film recorder

Magnetic tape stretches easily. This would ruin the synchronization so the sound is transferred to magnetic film. The tape recording is played back down a cable to a magnetic film recorder. This records the sound in the same way as the tape recorder did. The speed of the tape is precisely controlled by the sync pulses, which are now in a special sync unit. This ensures that the magnetic film recording is in perfect sync with the picture film. The sound film can now be edited.

4 Every location has its own particular background sound atmosphere. Wherever shooting takes place, a short recording is made with everything quiet. The "silences" can then be used to fill any gaps in the dialogue. These recordings are called buzz tracks.

Camera special effects

Many special effects can be created during shooting by using the camera in a certain way. More spectacular effects can be created during processing at the film laboratories but those done in the camera are usually more realistic. This is because they are created directly on to one strip of film. Those done in the laboratories usually involve re-photographing and this can reduce the quality of the pictures. Here are some of the main types of camera effects. Others include using different lenses and altering the speed of the camera motor. Some camera effects can be produced quite easily even with an 8mm home movie camera.

Double exposures

If the same piece of film is exposed twice, one picture can be seen through another when the film is developed. For instance, if a shot is taken of a graveyard and then the film is rewound and an actor is filmed walking about in the graveyard, the effect of a ghost is produced.

Matte shots

A matte shot is one which is taken with part of the frame of film covered up so that it does not expose. A sheet of matte (non-shiny) black card or thin metal is cut to the right shape and put in the matte box at the front of the camera lens. The simplest type of matte is used to give the effect of looking through a keyhole or binoculars (shown here) and is called a fixed matte.

Split screens

This is the name for frames which are filmed in two stages using mattes. The technique is useful for creating shots of identical twins played by the same actor and for shots like this one of someone with a dangerous animal.

1 First, a matte is put into the matte box to black out part of the frame and the actor is filmed in the other part, acting to empty space.

2 The film is then rewound, the actor's part of the frame is blacked out and the animal is filmed in the unexposed area.

3 When the film is developed, the actor and animal appear together. The join between the two parts of the frame is designed to fall on a part of the set where it will not show up, in this case on the tree.

4 When the first part of the frame is being shot, the actor has to know exactly where it is possible to move without disappearing behind the matte; otherwise the finished shot may look like this.

5 Several takes may be needed to get the second half of the frame right. If the animal strays into the area which is now behind the matte, the shot is ruined.

6 The mattes must be positioned so that they match up exactly. The camera has to be completely still during shooting so they do not move in relation to each other.

Joke shots are sometimes produced using the split screen technique. Below you can see how the mattes have been used to produce a shot of a car disappearing behind a thin pillar.

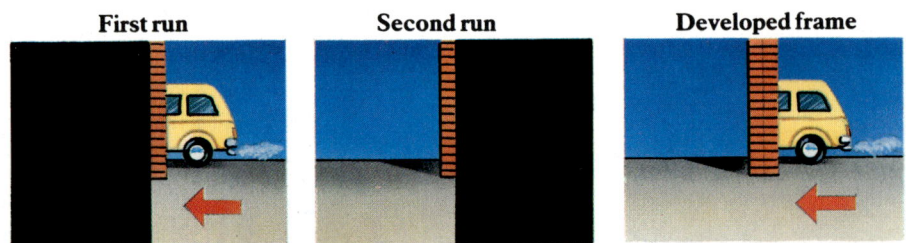

First run   Second run   Developed frame

Matte paintings

Sometimes a split screen shot is produced in which part of the frame is a real set or location and the other part is a painting. This is a useful way of transforming one landscape into another.

The first step is for the artist to set up a large sheet of glass in front of the camera and to paint out in black the part of the scene that needs to be changed.

The black area of the glass is then used as a matte and the action is filmed through the clear area. The actors have to stay directly behind the clear area or they are hidden from the camera by the black matte.

The artist then does a painting on another sheet of glass so that it corresponds exactly with the area blacked out on the original sheet. This time the actors' area appears black.

The film is run through the camera again and this time only the painting is shot. The real scene and the painting appear together in the developed picture.

Front projection

This is the name of a method often used to combine shots of actors or objects in a studio with a background scene filmed previously somewhere else. The pictures of the background scene are projected on to a screen while the foreground action takes place in front of it. The camera films both the foreground and the pictures on the screen at the same time. If the background pictures are moving, the audience can be tricked into believing that it is the foreground which is moving instead.

Types of shot often produced by front projection include those of astronauts in space. Here you can see how the technique works.

1 A projector beams pictures of outer space on to a mirror.

2 The mirror is positioned at such an angle (45° to the camera) that the pictures from the projector are reflected off it and on to the screen along the same line of sight as the camera's. This means that any shadows cast on the screen by the actors' bodies are hidden from the camera by the actors themselves.

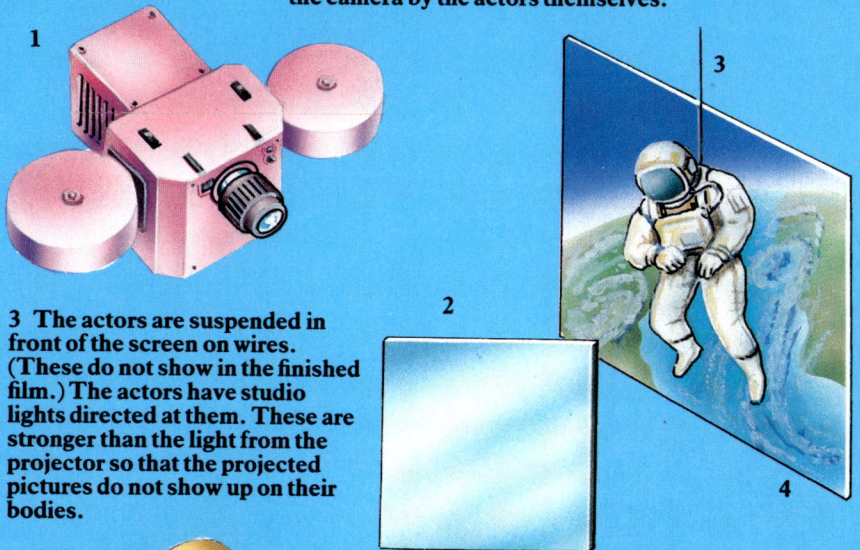

3 The actors are suspended in front of the screen on wires. (These do not show in the finished film.) The actors have studio lights directed at them. These are stronger than the light from the projector so that the projected pictures do not show up on their bodies.

4 The surface of the screen is covered with thousands of minute glass beads which reflect light in the direction from which it has come.

5 The mirror allows light to pass through it as well as reflecting light. The light from the screen and from the actors passes through it and into the camera. The camera photographs both the pictures on the screen and the actors in front of it.

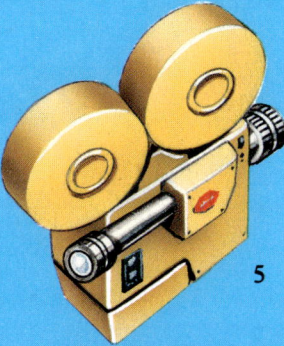

In a special type of front projection, zoom lenses are used on both the camera and projector. Here, for instance, the zoom on the camera enlarges the spacecraft so that it appears to come towards you. At the same time the zoom on the projector reduces the background. This counteracts the camera zoom and the background stays the same size in the combined shots.

In a film laboratory

Once the pictures have been shot, the film is taken out of the camera and sent to laboratories for processing. Film processing is a complex technical operation, which requires a lot of expensive equipment and very accurate control. Home movies, as well as feature films, are processed in laboratories.

At this stage no pictures are visible so the film is first put into special chemicals which develop them. The developed pictures are negatives of the original scene. Before the pictures can be projected, positives have to be made. These are produced by printing the negatives on to another piece of film. When this is developed, positive pictures appear. The positives can be projected on to a cinema screen to create a likeness of the original scene.

Developing

1 Film is sent to the laboratories in light-proof cans and is developed in a darkroom so the pictures cannot be spoilt by being exposed to light a second time. The film travels through the developing machine on a long system of rollers after being loaded on to the "pre-run" cabinet.

2 In the developer tank a solution of chemicals acts on the silver halide crystals which were exposed and changed as the film passed through the camera. This chemical action makes the pictures become visible.

Printing

The negatives are printed to make positives by being photographed on to another piece of light-sensitive film. There are two main methods of film printing.

In contact printing, which is the most usual method, the negatives are put in contact with the raw film and light is shone through them. No lens is used.

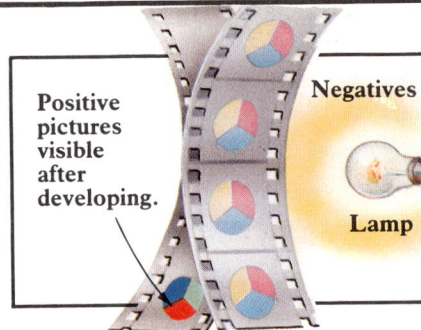

Positive pictures visible after developing.

Negatives

Lamp

Projector

Negatives in here.

Camera

Raw film in here.

In optical printing the negatives are put into a special high-quality projector and the raw film is put into a camera facing it. The projector light shines the negative pictures on to the film through a lens. The lens makes it possible to reduce or enlarge the pictures during printing and to produce various special effects. You can find out about these on pages 18-19.

Negatives and positives

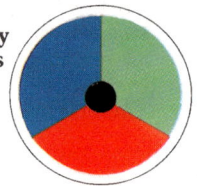

Primary colours

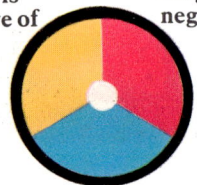

Yellow is negative of blue.

Magenta is negative of green.

Cyan is negative of red.

Black and white original.

Black and white negative.

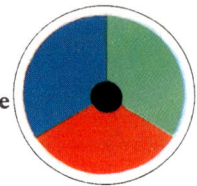

Positive

3 The film may still have some unexposed silver halide crystals on it. "Fixing" chemicals in the fixer tank remove them so that the pictures will not alter when they are taken out of the darkroom.

4 Water removes any remaining unwanted chemicals in the washing tank. This ensures that the pictures will not fade or change colour.

5 Streams of warm air dry the film in the drying cabinet and it is then unloaded from the machine.

There are three basic or "primary" colours of light: blue, green and red. All the other colours you see are made up of different combinations and proportions of these three.

The light-sensitive silver halide crystals on colour film are arranged in three separate layers. Each layer is sensitive to blue, green or red light. When the exposed film is developed, each layer produces a dye of the negative or "complementary" colour to the one which was reflected on to it from the original scene. The brighter the colour in the original, the deeper the dye on the negative.

You cannot really see this effect on colour negatives because, for technical reasons, they are covered with an orange masking. If you look at black and white negatives, though, you can see that the lightest parts of the original come out darkest on the negatives and vice versa.

The type of light in printing machines and projectors is "white" light, which contains all three primary colours. When the light is shone through the negatives in printing, the dyes on them act as a series of filters. The colours produced on the positives look the same as those in the original. When light is shone through the positives in the cinema projector the colours appear in their original form on the screen.

Colour grading

Before being printed the negatives are checked for any minor variations in colour or exposure from shot to shot. They are put on a machine called a colour analyser, which converts the negative pictures to positive on a TV screen. By adjusting the controls on the machine, the colour grader can vary the amounts of blue, green and red light in the pictures until they look right. These light settings are then recorded on punched tape or disc and are transferred to the printing machine so that the colours are corrected automatically during printing. The colours can also be deliberately distorted for effect.

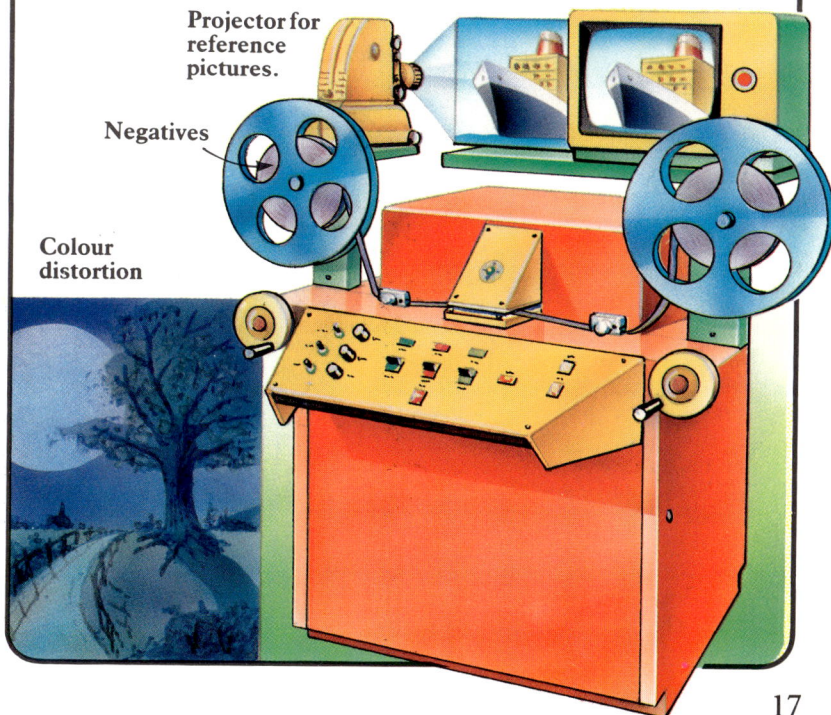

Projector for reference pictures.

Negatives

Colour distortion

Laboratory special effects

Most laboratory special effects are produced during printing on an optical printing machine. This is the machine which has a projector and a camera facing each other (see page 16). While the original, developed film is being run through the projector and re-photographed by the camera, various changes can be made to the pictures.

Effects produced on the optical printer are often referred to as "opticals". Some of them are very similar to effects created in the camera. For example, many split screen shots are produced in the laboratories. Instead of the matte consisting of a piece of partly black card in front of the camera lens, it is a piece of partly black film which is put in front of the film running through the printer's camera. Here are some examples of optical effects.

Fades and dissolves

These are produced using the shutter on the optical printer's camera. If the shutter is gradually closed during re-photographing, the picture fades out over a number of frames. If the shutter starts off closed and is gradually opened, the picture fades in. To make one picture change, or "dissolve", into another, like the globe above, a fade-out of the first picture is produced, then the film in the camera is rewound and a fade-in of the new picture is printed over the top.

Enlarging and reducing

Normal picture

Enlargement

Reduction

By moving the camera further away from the projector or nearer to it, the picture can be enlarged or reduced, as shown in the illustrations above.

This is the way 16mm films are converted to 35mm and vice versa. If the camera is moved while re-photographing is taking place, a zoom effect is produced. If a zoom-out is carried to extremes, the edge of the original frame comes into view and the picture shrinks into the distance.

Multiple images

If the camera is moved or "shifted" up, down or sideways, it is possible to re-position a reduced picture in the printed frame. A frame containing several different pictures can be built up in stages. One reduced picture is projected into a corner of the frame, the film in the camera is re-wound and the next picture is projected into another corner, and so on. Mattes are used to prevent the pictures being exposed twice in the camera and to crop the frames to the right shape.

Changing speed

Short sections of action are often speeded up by missing out some of the frames during printing. For example, a fall can be speeded up to make it look more exciting, while the rest of the action is kept at normal speed. By printing some frames more than once, the action can be slowed down. If it is slowed to less than half its original speed, the effect is not normal slow motion but a series of steps. When one frame is printed many times over, a "freeze frame" is produced. These are often used as a background for the title or credits of a film.

Backward motion

If the projector is run backwards instead of forwards, the pictures are printed in reverse order. This is sometimes done to produce joke shots of, for example, people diving upwards, cars going backwards or torn paper becoming whole.

Wipes

These are a type of split screen. The dividing line between the matte and the clear area of the frame is in a slightly different position in each successive frame. The line moves across the screen, wiping off one picture as another appears.

Travelling mattes

When the shape of a matte changes from one frame to the next, it is described as "travelling". Travelling mattes are useful for inserting shots of people or objects into a separately filmed moving background. Below you can see how the travelling matte technique can be used to produce shots of Santa Claus's sleigh flying over roof-tops. The same types of shots can be produced using the front projection technique described on page 15.

The roof-tops which are to form the background are filmed from an aeroplane.

Santa Claus and his sleigh are filmed in a studio against a bright blue screen.

The sleigh is printed on to special black and white film to produce two silhouettes, one black and one clear. These act as mattes.

The negative of the roof-tops is run through the printer's projector and shone on to the film in the camera.

The matte with the sleigh in black is put in front of the film in the camera. No light can get through the black part.

The result is a print of the roof-tops with an unexposed area the exact shape of the sleigh.

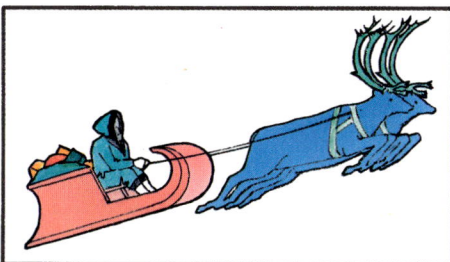

Next, the ordinary, colour negative of the sleigh is put through the projector and the film in the camera is rewound.

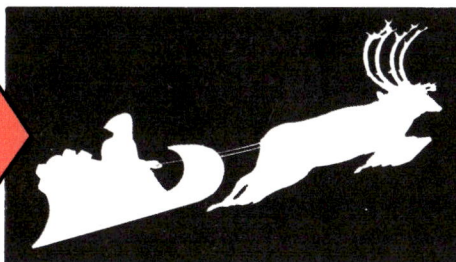

The other matte is put in front of the camera film to prevent the already printed background being exposed twice.

The sleigh is printed precisely into the patch of film which was unexposed on the first run.

Using models

Most major studios have special model shops where all the models needed for a film are made. In general, the nearer a model is to full-size the more realistic it looks on the screen. For practical and financial reasons though, many models are made in miniature and a lot of skill goes into making them convincing. Models of objects that exist in real life have to be made to look exactly like the original, right down to signs of wear and tear.

Models and live action can be combined in the same shot using a variety of techniques. These include split screens, front projection and blue screen travelling mattes. They can also be combined using an animation camera (see pages 22-23).

Monsters

Monsters are often played by actors in costume but the alternative is to build a model. First of all, a metal skeleton or "armature" is made, with moveable joints. The body is then modelled round the armature, usually in clay, and is covered with a flexible rubber or plastic skin. Any hair needed is stuck on.

For simple movements the monsters can be operated by remote control, but producing more complicated actions is a laborious process. The position of the monster has to be altered slightly by hand before every single frame of film is exposed (24 times for one second of screen time).

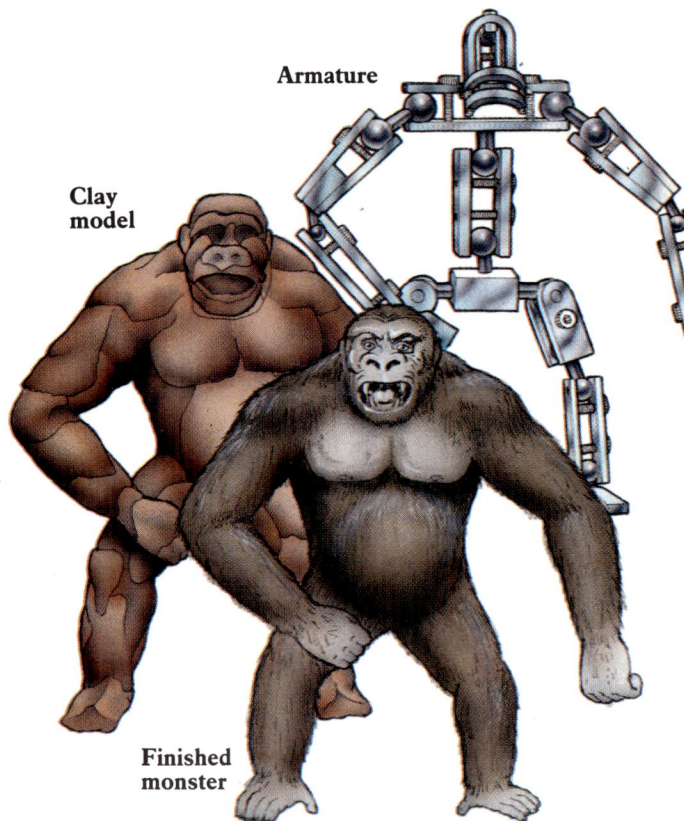

Armature

Clay model

Finished monster

People

It is even possible to use models, sometimes miniatures, of people, for instance as corpses, in certain crowd scenes, or in shots involving danger like this one. The models are never shown in close up and the camera makes lots of cuts away from them to live action.

Filming models

Many models are filmed using a method called motion control. In motion control filming, the camera is operated by computer. This means that the camera's movements can be repeated precisely several times over for a technique called "multi-pass" motion control. Here is an example of how the technique might be used. It can take several hours to produce a shot of a spaceship crossing the screen.

Model

Camera

Developed frame

Computer

1 The camera tracks slowly and smoothly past a model spacecraft. The camera is fitted with motors to control panning and tilting, and to drive the focus and zoom controls on the lens. The motors are controlled by signals from a computer. The spacecraft is also fitted with motors. These can be used to alter its position during the shot, to make it look as though the pilot is manoeuvring violently for example. The spacecraft is brightly lit but the windows are covered with black so they do not expose on the film.

Towns and landscapes

Miniatures of towns and landscapes are especially useful for disaster movies, where it would be impossible to arrange large-scale destruction by phenomena such as earthquakes. Miniatures of real places are among the most difficult to make convincing because of the amount of detail which has to be reproduced exactly. The camera seldom rests on this type of miniature for more than a few seconds without cutting to a large-scale model or to some live action.

Sometimes a miniature is combined with a full-size set or a real location by being suspended into the top part of the shot. It is then known as a "hanging miniature".

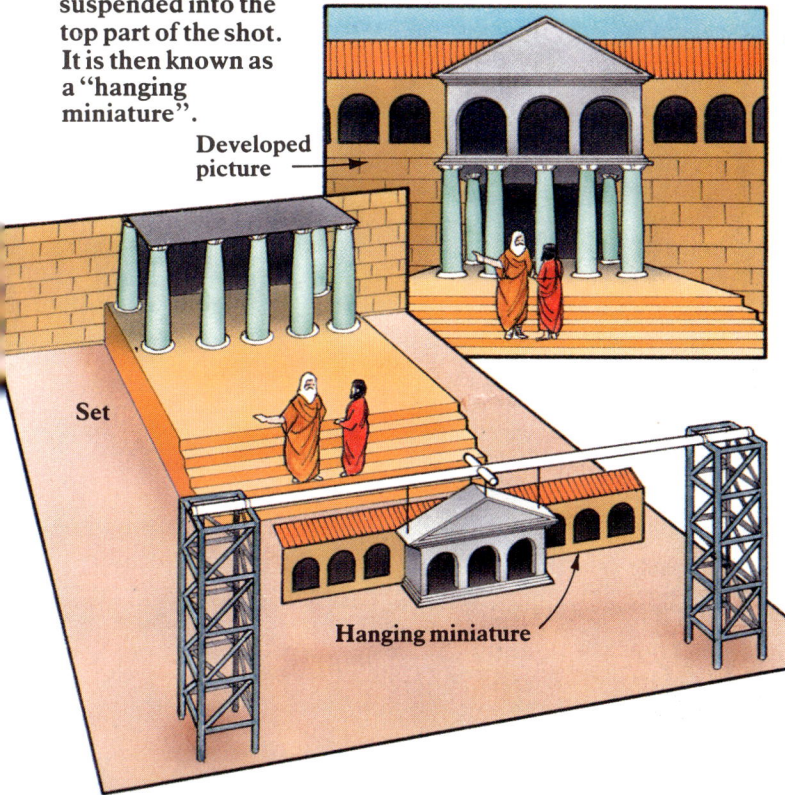

Developed picture

Set

Hanging miniature

Vehicles

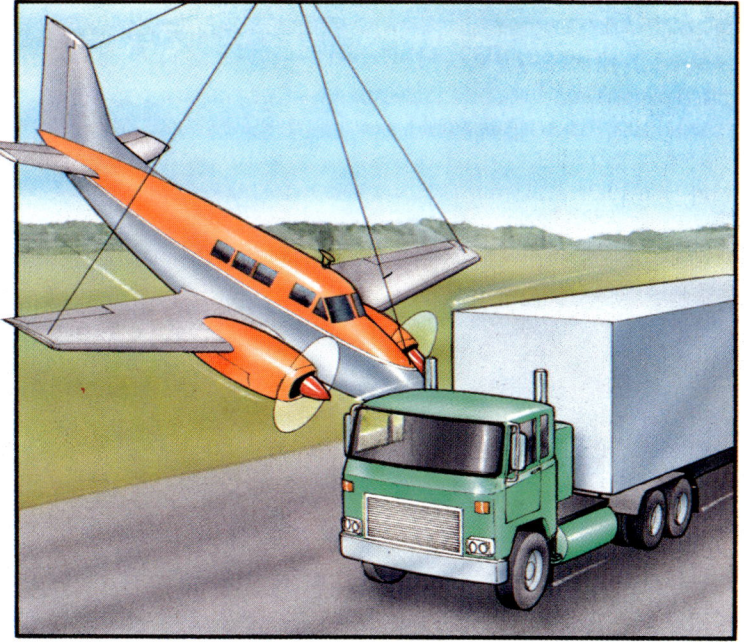

The spacecraft you see in science fiction films are really specially constructed models. Parts from model aircraft kits are often used in making miniature spacecraft.

Models of other types of vehicles are often used in war films or wherever lots of crashes or explosions are needed. Aeroplane crashes like the one shown above can be done by suspending a large-scale model of the plane on wires from a tall crane. The model is made of light, fragile material, such as balsa wood. It is pre-broken and then lightly glued back together so it breaks up easily on impact. It may also contain explosives, rigged to go off on impact.

Water cannot be miniaturized convincingly, so models of ships are made as large as possible and are filmed in the tank on the lot, on lakes or even on the sea.

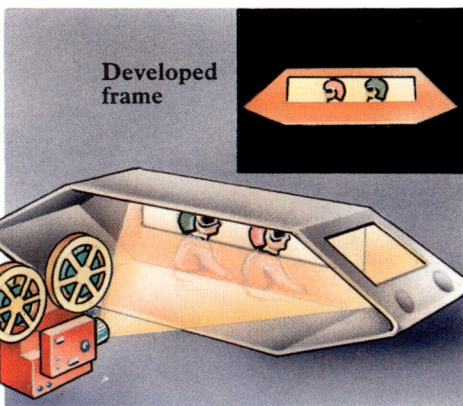

Developed frame

2 The film is wound back to the start of the shot and a second pass is made. This time the main lighting is switched off and a small projector shines pictures of cabin interiors and people on to the spacecraft windows from behind. The patches of film that were unexposed on the first pass are now exposed with these pictures.

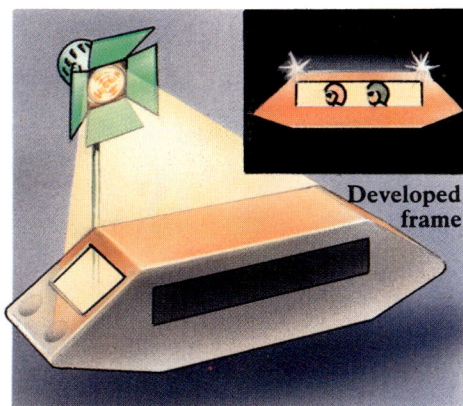

Developed frame

3 On the third pass only certain parts of the model are lit. This gives it shiny highlights, which can make it appear to glint as it manoeuvres.

Sometimes as many as six or seven passes are made for one shot. The model may then be given a background of stars using the animation camera in the animation studio.

Periscope lens

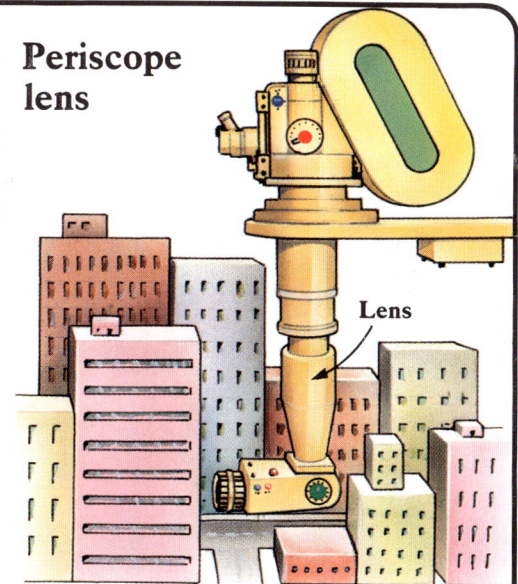

Lens

The motion control camera is sometimes fitted with a long periscope lens. This is useful for taking ground level shots in, say, a miniature city.

Animated films

Animated films are made possible because of the way in which all films consist of a succession of still photographs. For an animated cartoon film, photographs are taken of a series of drawings. If a character or object differs slightly in its position from one drawing to the next, it appears to move, or be "animated", when the photographs are projected. Animation is a very laborious process. If the movement is to look natural on the screen, 24 frames have to be projected every second in the usual way. This means that a cartoon lasting only ten minutes has to have thousands of drawings.

Drawing the pictures

1 First of all, an artist, known as an animator, draws the moving character frame by frame in pencil on separate sheets of paper. Each drawing is done with the previous one illuminated beneath it, so it is easier to make the changes from frame to frame accurately.

2 The drawings are photographed by a TV camera, the signals from the camera are stored in a computer and the animator checks that the movement of the character is correct by displaying the drawings on a screen. They can be displayed in any order and at different speeds.

3 After any corrections have been made to the drawings, each one is traced on to a separate sheet of transparent film, known as a cel, in black ink. The outline is then painted in. If a large part of the character's body is to be the same in several frames, this part may be done on one cel and only the moving parts, such as the arms and legs, on separate cels.

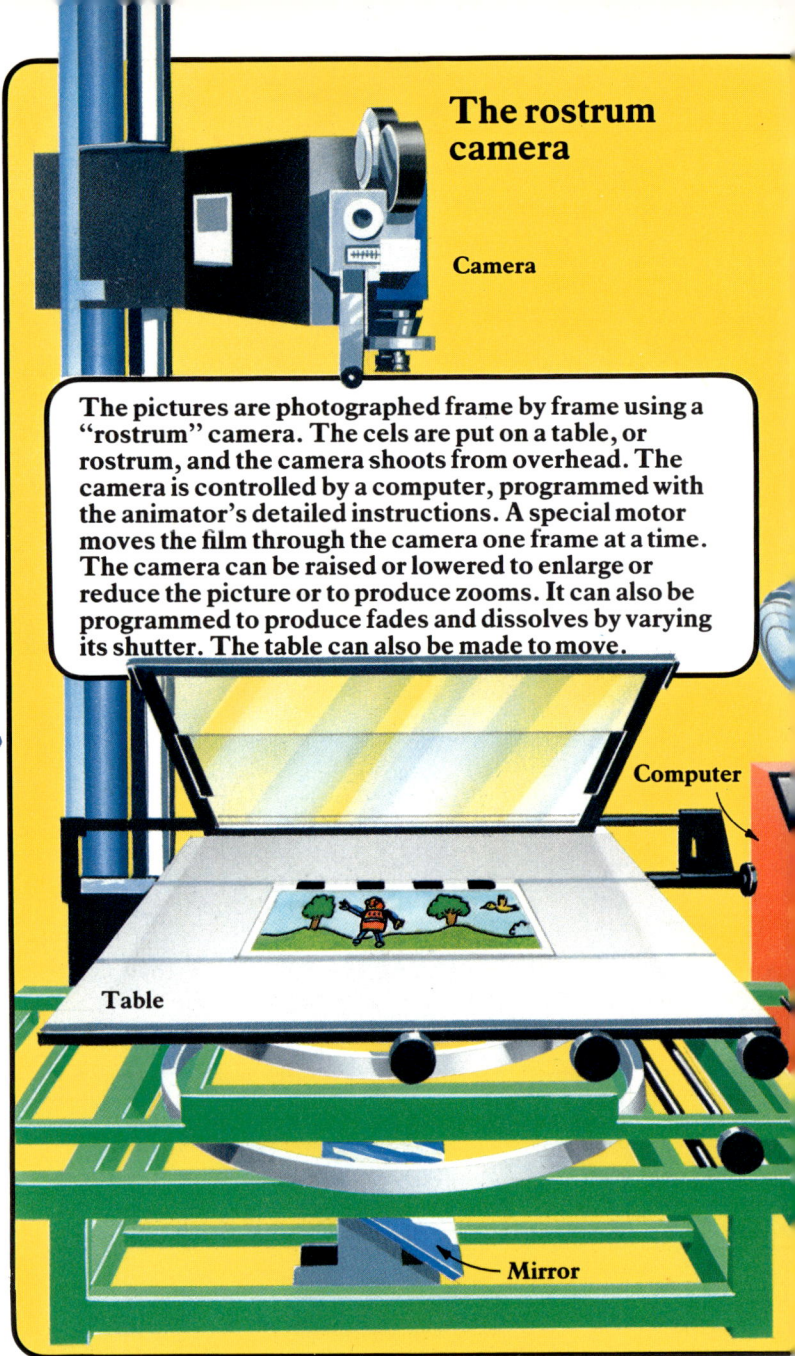

The rostrum camera

Camera

The pictures are photographed frame by frame using a "rostrum" camera. The cels are put on a table, or rostrum, and the camera shoots from overhead. The camera is controlled by a computer, programmed with the animator's detailed instructions. A special motor moves the film through the camera one frame at a time. The camera can be raised or lowered to enlarge or reduce the picture or to produce zooms. It can also be programmed to produce fades and dissolves by varying its shutter. The table can also be made to move.

Computer

Table

Mirror

4 The background is painted separately. If the camera is going to pan across it, the picture has to be very wide. Anything which is to appear in front of the main character, as foreground, is also painted on separate cels.

The cels needed for each frame are put on the table in layers and held flat by a glass plate. The plate can be lifted up after each shot for the cels to be replaced or adjusted as necessary. Each frame is usually photographed twice. This halves the number of set-ups needed and the repetition is not noticeable on the screen.

First exposure
Foreground cel
Body
Arms and legs
Background

Second exposure
New foreground cel with bird's wings in different position.
New cel for arms and legs.
Same cel for body.

Background moved to left so character appears to move to right.

Projector

Computer animation

Computers can do the drawings for some cartoons but they are still not used a great deal for this. Large, powerful computers are needed and they are expensive and slow-working.

An animator touches different spots on the computer screen with a special pen. The computer is programmed to draw lines between the spots and to fill in areas of colour. Sometimes the animator produces only the key frames and the computer works out the in-between ones automatically.

The objects in the pictures can be altered by the computer. They can be squashed or stretched, bent, rotated, broken up and reassembled, or their colours can be changed. The computer can also produce more conventional effects such as fades, zooms and multiple images.

Good quality photographs cannot be produced by filming the colour screen. The pictures are transferred to a black and white TV screen, one primary colour at a time. Each of the three "colours" is then photographed on to one frame of film through a blue, green or red filter to build up a full colour picture.

Combining cartoons and people

A cartoon character can be made to appear in the same shot as an actor, using the rostrum camera. Shots of the actor are projected from below the table, the animation cels are put on top and the camera films both together. The shots have to be carefully planned so that they match up.

Object animation

It is possible to animate objects as well as drawings simply by re-positioning them slightly between frames. This is the way monster models are made to move. The technique is often used in advertisements. A bar of chocolate can be made to glide around as if by magic, or even to unwrap itself.

23

Stunts

When a shot involving danger cannot be faked convincingly by using a special effects technique, professional stunt artists are called in to double for the actors. Skilled technicians, such as ammunition experts, set up the stunts so that they are no more dangerous than is absolutely necessary.* The stunt artists must be at the peak of fitness and prepare carefully for every stunt. Not all the work they do involves risking their lives. Sometimes they just have to do running sequences so there is no possibility of shooting being delayed by a leading actor spraining an ankle.

"Breakaway" wheel

Dummy driver

Compressed air cannon

Cars

Stunt artists are used to drive cars in chase sequences and for manoeuvres such as skids and near-misses. Both the driver's body and the interior of the car are well padded. If a car has to collide or turn over, a dummy driver is used. Cars can be made to crash in various ways. They can be operated by remote control, or be towed by fine wires which will not be seen on the screen, or they can be catapulted into the crash by a compressed air or steam cannon. There are often explosives in the car, rigged to burst into flames on impact.

Falls

Shattering plastic

There are two main ways of breaking a high fall. One is to attach a nylon rope to the stunt artist and choose the angle of the shot carefully so it is not seen in the picture. The other is to cushion the fall with air bags or, as shown here, with empty cardboard boxes and soft mattresses. Next time you see a high fall in a film, notice how the camera cuts away just before the impact. To minimize the risk of injury, fall artists try to land on their backs and shoulders in a slightly jack-knifed position. Even for simple falls, they wear padding under their clothes·

Fire

The trick of creating fire in films is to make maximum use of smoke, produced by a smoke machine, and flickering effects supplied by a flame drum. The flames themselves are often produced by "fire forks". These are linked up to gas cylinders and the size of the flames is controlled by valves. More spectacular flames can be made for a large-scale fire by burning a metal frame covered with material soaked in petrol. The sets and props are often made of flameproof material so they do not get burnt up and can be used again if a re-take is necessary. When a person has to be shown on fire, extremely strict safety precautions are taken. The stunt artist wears a fireproof suit which is fitted with its own air supply beneath a mask of the actor's face.

Flameproof set

Flame drum

Smoke machine

Fire fork

*Without professional training all stunts are extremely dangerous. Don't try to imitate any of the ones described here.

Weapons

Real weapons are usually used in films only for still close-ups. The guns you see people carrying around are generally replicas or at least have major components missing. If an actor has to be seen shooting, a special gun for firing blanks is used.

Electric detonators are often used as bullets. A small detonator is put in a bag of artificial blood and fitted under the stunt artist's clothes. When the detonator goes off, it ruptures the blood bag and blows a hole in the clothes.

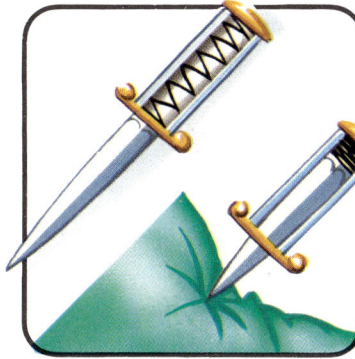

Knives are usually made of rubber or foam plastic. For stabbings, ones with retractable blades are used. (The blade disappears into the handle on impact.) The handle is sometimes fitted with a piston which pumps artificial blood to the point of the knife.

The arrows you see in films are sometimes pop-up ones. They are concealed in channels in a shield and have a spring attached at the back. When the stunt artist releases the spring, the arrows pop up so fast nobody realizes they have moved in the wrong direction.

Explosions

Real explosions are usually made only in the open air. They are known as pyrotechnics or "pyros", which means fireworks. They include thunderflashes, which are like large "bangers" and maroons, which produce more violent explosions, throwing earth and dust into the air. The explosives can be combined with petrol to make flames. For a battlefield scene, maroons are buried in precisely marked spots and the movements of the actors and stunt artists are carefully plotted out and timed so that nobody is directly on top of one when it goes off.

For indoor explosions the flash and smoke are made by special, safe "flash powder" and the furniture is thrown around and broken mechanically. Many stunt props are made of lightweight, fragile materials which do not produce dangerous splinters and can even be smashed over people's heads. They are known as "breakaways". Below you can see how a bomb explosion in a cupboard might be faked. All the devices are wired to a single button.

Lightweight cupboard. Sides are not fixed together but held together by nylon cords inside. Detonators on the cords break them at the right moment.

Window made of shattering plastic. Curtains and papers will be blown about by compressed air cylinders hidden from camera.

Breakaway glass and bottle made of plaster, wax or brittle plastic. Detonators inside make them shatter.

Stunt artist attached to one wall of set by taut nylon cord fitted with detonator and to other wall by taut elastic. When detonator breaks cord, elastic pulls him off chair.

Strong elastic attached to set makes cupboard fly apart.

The "bomb" is really flash powder in this metal box called a flash pan.

Breakaway chair made of balsa wood or rigid foam plastic. Frame may be pre-broken and only lightly glued together again.

Editing and printing

Before a film can be printed and distributed to cinemas, all the shots filmed at different times and in different places have to be put together in the right order and the soundtracks have to be incorporated. This is the responsibility of the editor, who works closely with the director. The best takes of the different scenes are chosen, certain scenes are cut if necessary and the order of shots may be altered from the one given in the script. The effect the film has on the audience depends a great deal on the editing.

1 Assembly

Film bin

Picture synchronizer

Guillotine

Sticky tape

Film joiner

The first stage in editing the film is for the editor and director to view the prints made after each day's shooting and to listen to the dialogue recording, which is on magnetic film. The pictures and sound are synchronized by matching the picture of the clapstick striking the clapperboard with the sound the stick makes on the soundtrack. These "rushes" or "dailies" are then used as the editor's work print or "cutting copy". They are cut into individual shots and hung up over a "film bin". A linen bag in the bin helps to prevent damage to the loose ends. The editor then assembles both the pictures and dialogue in script order. A machine called a picture synchronizer is used for viewing the pictures and playing back the dialogue recording. A "film joiner" is used for making the cuts in the film and for sticking the ends together with transparent sticky tape.

2 Editing

Much of the editing is done on an editing machine, which gives better picture and sound reproduction than a picture synchronizer. The film can be wound backwards or forwards either fast or slow. The dialogue recording is edited at the same time as the pictures and the two are kept carefully in sync. Any special effects shots produced in the laboratories are incorporated at this stage, and any animation sequences. None of the unused shots or "trims" (parts of shots) is thrown away. They are all carefully logged and filed away in film cans.

Dialogue

Pictures

Film joiner

3 Track laying

The rest of the soundtracks, such as effects and music, are now edited and synchronized with the pictures and dialogue. The tracks are laid out alongside the pictures and dialogue on the picture synchronizer. A cue sheet, giving details of how the tracks line up with each other, is prepared for the sound mixing department.

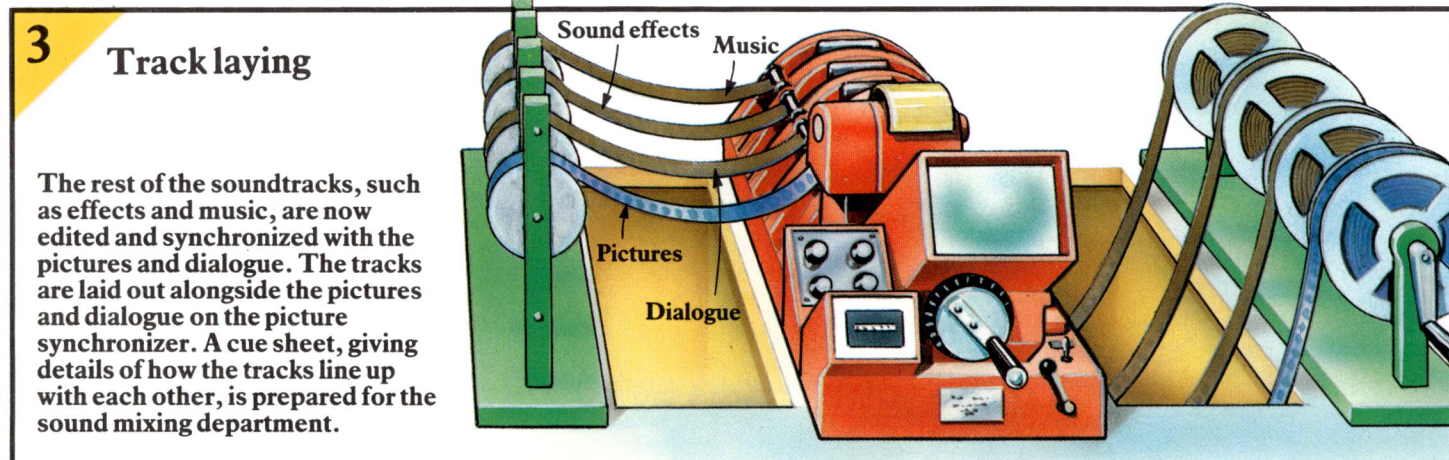

Sound effects

Music

Pictures

Dialogue

4 Sound mixing

Echo unit →

Fader

Mixing desk

Magnetic film recorder

Film counter

Playback machines

In the mixing studio all the different soundtracks are played back and the sound signals are fed to the mixing desk. A sound engineer watches the pictures on a screen and, following the instructions on the editor's cue sheet, mixes the tracks into one master track. This is recorded on a magnetic film recorder.

Each track is played back on a separate machine and has its own channel on the mixing desk. By moving the channels' fader controls the engineer can adjust the volume of the track. Effects such as echo and distortion can be added. Any completely new effects can be mixed in from a record player or tape deck. If the sound is to be in stereo, a "pan pot" control is used to split the signals into two on the master track.

5 Optical sound recording

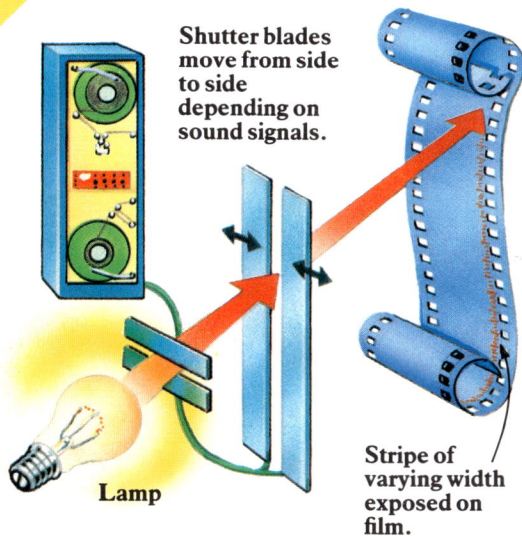

Shutter blades move from side to side depending on sound signals.

Lamp

Stripe of varying width exposed on film.

The master soundtrack is now transferred from magnetic film to photographic film, of the same type as is used for the pictures. This is done in an "optical sound camera". A playback machine is linked up to the shutter of the camera and the sound is played. As the sound signals vary, the width of the shutter opening varies. This means that as photographic film passes behind the shutter, a stripe of varying widths is exposed along it. (There are two stripes for a stereo recording.) The sound is now stored as a photographic pattern instead of a magnetic pattern. The film is developed to produce an optical sound negative.

6 Negative cutting

The picture negatives have been stored safely away. Now they are cut to match the edited work print. A "film splicer" is used for making the cuts and for joining the ends together with a special adhesive known as film cement. The negative cutters work in special dust-free conditions and wear cotton gloves to help protect the negatives.

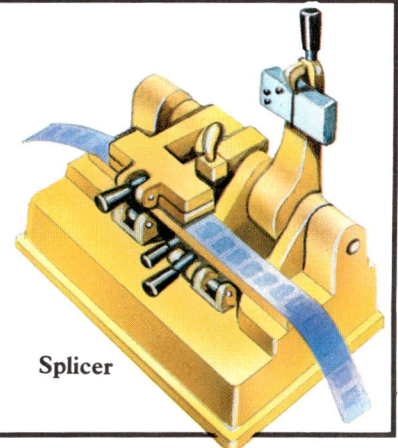

Splicer

7 Printing★

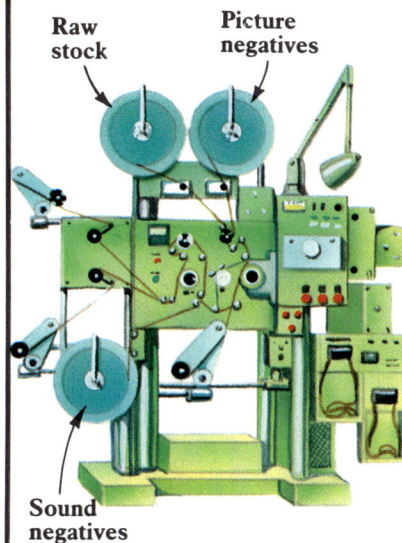

Raw stock

Picture negatives

Sound negatives

The picture negatives are colour graded at the laboratories. Now they and the optical sound negative are ready to be printed on to one piece of film. Either a contact printing machine, like the one on the left, or an optical printing machine is used. The first print to have pictures and sound combined is called the first married print or answer print. After being developed so the pictures and soundtracks become visible, the film is given a final check by the director, editor and grader. A duplicate negative is made from the master negatives, which are then stored safely away. Identical copies, called release prints, are made from the duplicate negative and are distributed to cinemas.

★See pages 16-17 for more about printing.

In the cinema

Since the establishment of television in the 1950s and video in the early 1980s, the cinema industry has produced increasingly spectacular films to try and keep its audiences. The quality of both film pictures and sound has improved.

How a projector works

A projector works rather like a camera in reverse. A camera lens focuses a tiny picture on to a piece of film inside it. The picture is developed and printed on to another piece of film and this is put into the projector. The projector lens focuses the picture on to a screen. Different types of projector project different widths of film. The projector shown here is for 35mm film.

1 The film is drawn through the projector from this feed reel, usually at the rate of 24 frames a second.

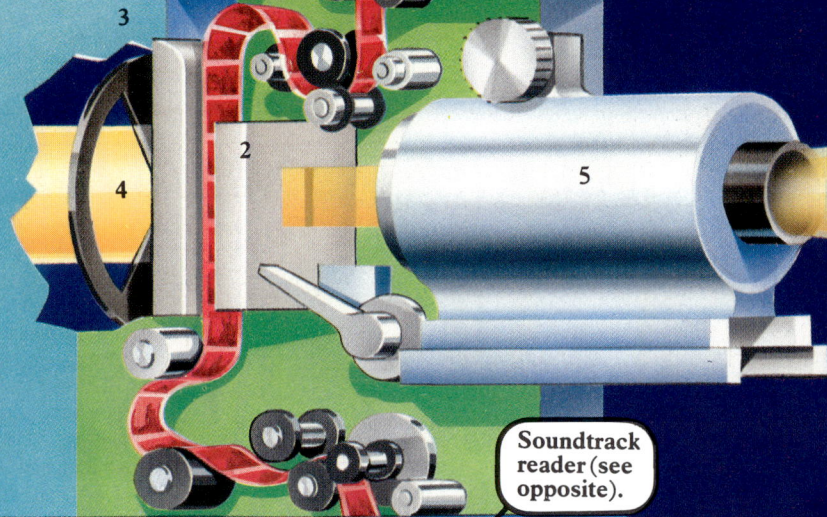

2 The frames are pulled down one by one into the gate of the projector, which is similar to the gate of a camera. Each frame is held steady in the gate for a fraction of a second.

3 As each frame is stationary in the gate, a shutter behind the gate opens.

4 When the shutter is open, an extremely powerful lamp shines on to the film in the gate.

5 The light travels from the film through a lens in front of the gate. The lens enlarges the picture on the film and focuses it on to the cinema screen. The screen has a highly reflective surface so the picture can be seen clearly. Like a camera lens, a projector lens inverts the picture, so the film is put into the projector upside down.

Soundtrack reader (see opposite).

6 The film collects on the take-up reel.

Changing reels

A film lasting 150 minutes is 13,500ft (4,114m) long and would need a reel almost a metre in diameter to hold it all. For this reason most cinemas have two projectors working alternately, each showing reels lasting about 20 minutes. You may sometimes see a dot flashing in the top right-hand corner of the screen. This is a "cue dot", signalling that one reel is about to run out and the other projector has to take over.

Look for cue dot here.

Screens

Cinemas have wide screens so that they can show films made using a system called "scope". Scope films are shot with a special lens on the camera. This squeezes the pictures at the sides to fit more in. On the film everything looks very tall and thin but a special lens on the projector unsqueezes the picture again and spreads it on to the wide screen. Non-scope films have to be projected with the top and bottom cut off in order to fit the height of the screen. This is allowed for during shooting.

Scope film on screen.

Non-scope film on screen.

Scope film

70mm film

It is worth going to see 70mm films if you have the chance. The pictures do not have to be enlarged by the projector as much as standard 35mm ones do. This means that they are much sharper. The quality of the sound is also better and there is more room on the film for extra soundtracks (see below).

Imax

63ft (19m)

52ft (16m)

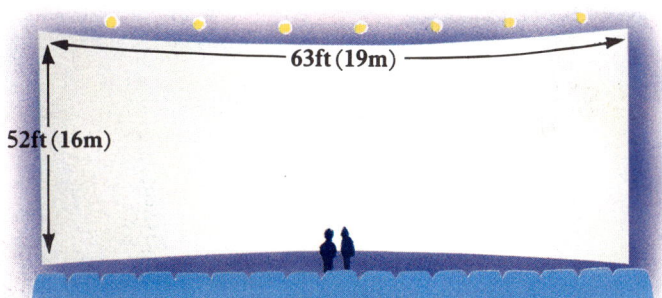

This is the name of a system in which exceptionally high-quality pictures are projected on to a huge curved screen which fills the whole of the audience's field of vision. Extra-large cameras and projectors have to be used because the frames of film are ten times larger than 35mm frames. The system is not yet in general use.

3D films

Audience sees this.

The pictures of three-dimensional (3D) films appear to come out of the screen towards the audience. The films are usually made by shooting each scene with two separate cameras. The distance between the cameras' lenses is similar to that between people's eyes. The two sets of prints are projected on to the screen at the same time. The audience has to wear special glasses with filters so that they see one picture with the left eye and the other with the right.

Soundtrack reading

1 On its way through the projector, the film goes past a soundtrack reader. This works by shining a light through the sound stripe printed down the edge of the film. The width of the sound stripe varies according to the sound signals that were produced during recording. This means that a varying amount of light passes through it. A device called a photoelectric cell converts the varying amount of light into sound signals. These are identical to the original sound signals. They travel down a cable to the cinema's loudspeakers, which convert them into audible sound waves. If a film has two sound stripes for stereo sound, the projector has to have two soundtrack readers side by side, one for each stripe.

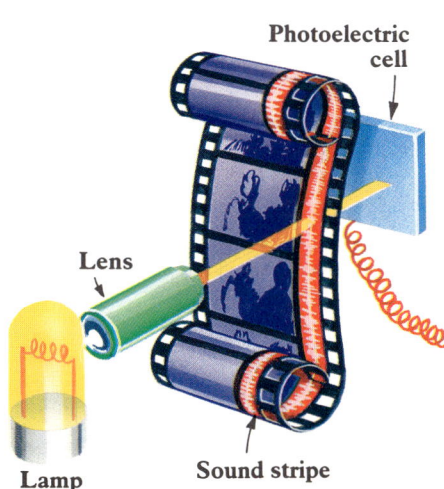

Photoelectric cell

Lens

Lamp

Sound stripe

2 The soundtrack reader is positioned below the gate of the projector. This means that a sound has to be printed further along the film than the picture it accompanies, otherwise the pictures and sound do not synchronize.

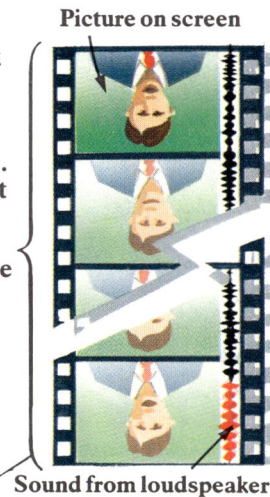

Picture on screen

Sound from loudspeaker

20 frames

Making home movies

The best way to get started in making your own films is to talk to experienced film-makers. Try asking at your local library whether there is a film club in your area. The club would have all the necessary equipment, which is expensive to buy. If you do want to buy your own equipment, have a really good look round the photographic shops before coming to a decision. You will find advertisements for equipment and suppliers in the home movie magazines. Read the manufacturers' publicity brochures carefully and ask as many people as possible for advice.

The type of camera and film usually used for home movies is called Super 8, because the film is 8mm wide. You can make interesting and varied films in Super 8, although advanced special effects, such as travelling mattes, are not possible.

Film

Sound stripe

If you want to record sound at the same time as you are shooting, you need to use "pre-striped" Super 8 film. This has a sound recording stripe down one edge. If you prefer to record a soundtrack after you have edited the pictures, you can buy silent film. Then you send it away to have the stripe put on it after editing. Even if you use pre-striped film, you can still do some editing of both pictures and sound.

The cheapest type of 8mm film to buy is called reversal film. This does not need to be printed on to another piece of film after developing but can be projected as it is. Black and white reversal film is quite hard to find.

Editing equipment and projectors

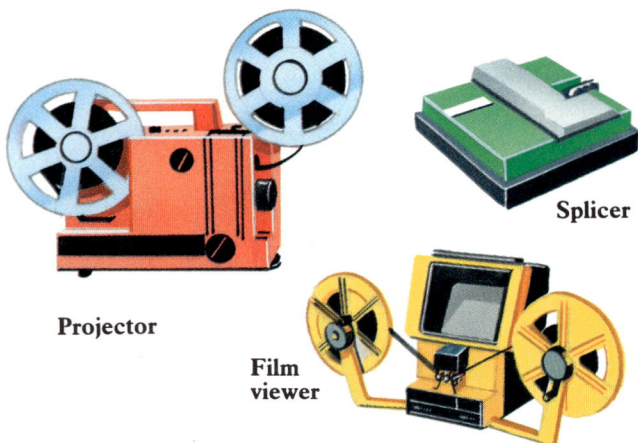

Splicer

Projector

Film viewer

It is not necessary to have a great deal of editing equipment. Photographic shops sell splicers for cutting and joining bits of film. A hand-wound film viewer is also useful though not essential. Like the cameras, Super 8 projectors come in a wide range of types and prices. Beginners often start off with a simple, two-speed, silent model, like the one below. You may find that you soon want to go on to a variable speed, reversible, silent model or a two-speed, sound model.

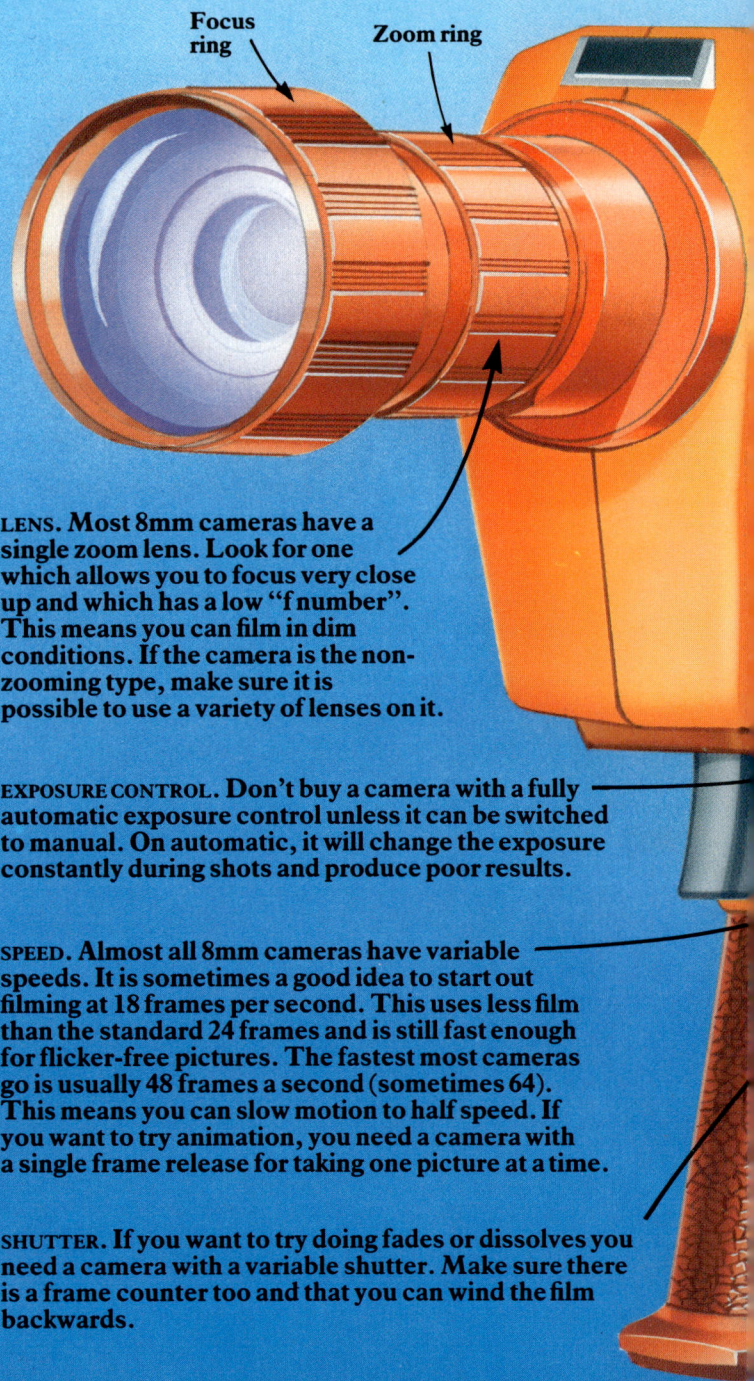

The camera

Super 8 cameras come in a wide range of models and prices. Here are just a few points to watch out for.

VIEWFINDER. Try to use a camera with a "reflex" viewfinder. This means that you get in the picture exactly what you see through the viewfinder.

Focus ring

Zoom ring

LENS. Most 8mm cameras have a single zoom lens. Look for one which allows you to focus very close up and which has a low "f number". This means you can film in dim conditions. If the camera is the non-zooming type, make sure it is possible to use a variety of lenses on it.

EXPOSURE CONTROL. Don't buy a camera with a fully automatic exposure control unless it can be switched to manual. On automatic, it will change the exposure constantly during shots and produce poor results.

SPEED. Almost all 8mm cameras have variable speeds. It is sometimes a good idea to start out filming at 18 frames per second. This uses less film than the standard 24 frames and is still fast enough for flicker-free pictures. The fastest most cameras go is usually 48 frames a second (sometimes 64). This means you can slow motion to half speed. If you want to try animation, you need a camera with a single frame release for taking one picture at a time.

SHUTTER. If you want to try doing fades or dissolves you need a camera with a variable shutter. Make sure there is a frame counter too and that you can wind the film backwards.

MICROPHONE. If the camera is fitted with a microphone, make sure it is removable so you can position it where you want.

SOUND RECORDING HEAD. This is necessary if you want to record sound, for example dialogue, at the same time as you shoot the pictures. You have to use pre-striped film (see opposite page) and will need a sound projector for playback.

Frame counter

Battery check button

MOTOR. Motors can be electric, like this one, or clockwork. You may find that an electric motor tends to run away with your film. On the other hand, you have to keep winding a clockwork motor up and it may stop in mid-shot.

Power on/off switch.

GRIP. All Super 8 cameras can be hand-held but you will achieve much better results if you use a tripod to rest the camera on whenever possible. Sequences that jump and jerk about are very hard to watch.

Camera shots

One of the best ways of learning how to make films, apart from talking to experts, is to watch as many films as you can very closely. If you can watch them on video at home, look at the same sequences several times over and notice how the shots have been put together.

Below are just a few basic shots you could try. Remember that a shot is whatever is filmed in one go, without stopping the camera. Always try and plan your shots in advance and work out how each one will lead into the next. Make sure that all your camera movements are slow and steady.

 Long shot
 Medium shot
 Close-up

You need to vary your shots to keep your audience's attention but if you jump from one viewpoint to another too quickly you will only confuse them. When you first start filming, it is a good idea to make each shot last about ten seconds. If you have a zoom lens, you can change the viewpoint in mid-shot as well as at the end. Don't be tempted to use the zoom as though it were a trombone.

 Normal lens
 Wide angle lens
 Telephoto lens

You can also vary your shots by using different lenses. Put very simply, a normal lens gives a picture of a scene much as you see it with the naked eye, a wide angle lens fits more in, and a telephoto lens gives an enlargement.

 Straight on
 High angle
 Low angle

Try to get variety by shooting from high and low angles as well as from straight on.

It is a good idea to hold the camera still for at least three seconds at the start and end of panning or tilting. Don't pan backwards and forwards repeatedly. This is known as hose-piping.

Index

First published in 1984 by Usborne Publishing Ltd, 20 Garrick Street, London WC2E 9BJ, England.

Copyright © 1984 Usborne Publishing Ltd.

The name Usborne and the device 🐝 are Trade Marks of Usborne Publishing Ltd.